GOD
of Becoming *and* Relationship

THE DYNAMIC NATURE
OF PROCESS THEOLOGY

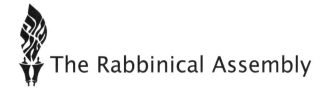

Study Guide

Rabbi Bradley Shavit Artson, DHL
and Nathan A. Roller

The Rabbinical Assembly

For People of All Faiths, All Backgrounds
JEWISH LIGHTS Publishing

T0145885

God of Becoming and Relationship Study Guide

2015 Paperback Edition, First Printing
©2015 Bradley Shavit Artson and Nathan A. Roller

For People of All Faiths, All Backgrounds
Published by Jewish Lights Publishing
www.jewishlights.com

Contents

Welcome!

Dear Instructor,

This study guide is designed to assist you in presenting the rich mixture of insights, ideas, and ethics distilled in the book *God of Becoming and Relationship: The Dynamic Nature of Process Theology.* In teaching this material, you will have a chance to help people work with what they know about the world from scientific and contemporary ideas to enrich their own spiritual development and gain new ways of understanding God, Torah, and morality. The blend of concepts that is Process Thought will also help them see deeper meaning in the Hebrew Bible and in the prayer book, allowing them to fashion a more meaningful relationship with Judaism and strengthen their own spiritual growth.

Each chapter of the book has its own section in this study guide. Key terms are listed and guiding questions will help you shape group conversation about the chapter. Additional texts with discussion questions will facilitate connecting new insights with Jewish tradition and the unique personalities and values of your students. Translations of biblical texts are taken from the Jewish Publication Society, and occasionally modified to be gender inclusive. Rabbinic translations are our own unless otherwise listed in the resources. For complete publication information on other sources we've quoted, please see the bibliography at the end of the guide.

Before you begin, make sure that all participants have their own copy of the book so they are able to read in advance, follow along during group discussion, and write their own questions, thoughts, and responses. Making the learning personal is always essential, but it is especially so when what you are teaching is a process of dynamism and relationship. The chapters vary in length, so you may wish to take two weeks to discuss longer chapters or combine two shorter chapters in one class session. This will depend on the group dynamic and the number of weeks you have for the class, of course, but you may find it helpful to plot out a tentative class schedule before the first session.

Prior to the first week, and for each class thereafter, *it is important that each student read the chapter that will be discussed before the next session.* That will give them the opportunity to go through the new material in advance on their own. You might ask them to jot down any terms they need to have clarified, any new ideas they find intriguing or troubling, and any topics they want to explore with the group. These lists of questions and thoughts will become a diary of spiritual exploration that can be a springboard for the entire group.

Before the first session of class meets, ask people to read in advance "A Father's Letter to His Son" (pp. 155–161) as a personal and passionate presentation of the core ideas that Process Thought makes possible. Ask them to jot down questions, notes, or responses to discuss during the first session.

I suggest for the first class that you focus on these responses. This would also be a good time to ask each person to share hopes or expectations for the class, and perhaps discuss what they know about Process Theology (if anything) and their general reactions to the idea of God and the universe as interconnected and continuously changing in a dynamic relationship.

As you teach this material, please feel free to avail yourself of the online resources found at the end of the book, and you are welcome to contact the author at bartson@aju.edu for further exploration or assistance.

Happy learning!
Rabbi Bradley Shavit Artson, DHL, and Nathan Andrew Roller

The Living, Luring God
Recovering a Biblically and Rabbinically Rooted Divine

In this chapter, Rabbi Artson introduces and then challenges the Greek inspired "dominant" theology (to use Rabbi Artson's term; this is often referred to as "classical" theology) that portrays God as eternal, unchanging, omnipotent, omniscient, and omnibenevolent. Rabbi Artson argues that not only are these axioms foreign to biblical and rabbinic Jewish understandings of God, but taken together they lead to "certain intolerable consequences" (p. 3) relating to evil and human freedom. Artson concludes by showing how Process Theology offers an understanding of God and the world that is more in line with Jewish conceptions and that avoids the intellectual and ethical pitfalls of the dominant theology.

Key Terms
- Omnipotent
- Omniscient
- Omnibenevolent
- Impassible

Discussion Questions
1. a) According to Rabbi Artson, what two problems arise from the assertion that God is all-powerful? (pp. 3–5)

   b) Why do such problems lead many to reject religion?

2. What does Rabbi Artson mean when he says "absolute power is self-erasing" (p. 4)?

3. How does the claim that God is all-knowing challenge the concept of human freedom? (pp. 5–6)

4. a) How does the conception of God as unchanging emerge from the axioms that God is omnipotent, omniscient, and omnibenevolent?

b) How does the text that Rabbi Artson brings from Berakhot 59a conflict with this view of God? (p. 6)

5. a) Why do some theologians "hide behind the term mystery" (p. 6)?

   b) Why is this not an acceptable solution according to Rabbi Artson?

Text Study

All the might, the praise, the greatness and the power belong to the Majesty of Majesties, yet God "loves law" (Exod. 21:1). It is the custom of the world that a powerful tyrant does not desire to do things lawfully, rather he bypasses law and order by coercing, stealing, transgressing the will of his Creator, favoring his friends and relatives while treating his antagonists unjustly. But the Holy Blessing One, the Majesty of all Majesties, "loves law," and does nothing unless it is with law. This is the meaning of "Mighty is the King who loves law."

> —Tanhuma, Mishpatim 1

In the first serious theological conversation I ever had with David Griffin, he said something wonderful that has remained with me ever since. He said, "Maybe God is all-powerful but God's power is not the power to coerce but the power to enable." In other words, God can do anything, but only through human and other instruments. I thought that was a remarkable insight, and responded by saying, "That's why, so often in the Bible and afterwards, God is portrayed by fire—at the Burning Bush, in the Eternal Flame before the Ark, etc." Fire is not an object: fire is a process, the process by which latent energy in a lump of coal or a log of wood is turned into actual energy. God is like fire, liberating the potential energy in each of us.

> — Rabbi Harold Kushner, "Would an All-Powerful God Be Worthy of Worship?" in *Jewish Theology and Process Thought*, p. 91

1. a) How do the Midrash Tanhuma and Rabbi Kushner understand God's power?

   b) How does each take what might be considered at first glance to be a limitation on God and instead turn that into an argument for God's strength?

2. How do these views fit with Rabbi Artson's understanding of God's limited power?

Reality and Relationship
Being a Creature in a Constantly Co-created Cosmos

Having demonstrated the shortcomings of the dominant metaphysical conception of God and the cosmos in the previous chapter, Rabbi Artson now explains the Process conception that reality is dynamic and relational. God, in this view, is in a partnership with the cosmos, and both have an active role in their own becoming.

Key Terms

- Agency
- Dipolarity
- Ontology
- Hyathology
- Novelty

Discussion Questions

1. a) What does Rabbi Artson mean when he says that reality is relational? (pp. 9–10)

   b) How is this concept connected to the Jewish concept of *brit*?

2. a) What does Rabbi Artson mean when he says that "we—and everything that exists—are events"? (p. 10)

   b) How does this lead to freedom being "an inherent quality of the world"? What are the limits of this freedom? Where does God fit into this framework? (pp. 10–12)

3. How do the rabbinic sources that Rabbi Artson brings to this chapter support the Process conception of God as dipolar? (pp. 12–14)

Text Study

Rabbi Eleazar discoursed on the text: "How great is your goodness which you have laid up for them that fear You, You have wrought for them that put their trust in You, before the children of people" (Ps. 31:20). Rabbi Eleazar said: "God created humanity in the world and gave them the faculty to perfect themselves in God's service and to direct their ways so as to merit the enjoyment of that celestial light which God has hidden and reserved for the righteous, as it is written, 'Eye has not seen, O Holy One, besides You, what You will do for one that waits for You' (Isa. 64:3). It is through the Torah that a person can become worthy of that light. For whoever studies Torah every day is earning a share in the future world, and is even accounted a builder of worlds, because through the Torah the world has been built and completed; so the Scripture says, 'The Holy One founded the earth with Wisdom (i.e., the Torah), and established the heavens with understanding' (Prov. 3:19), and again, 'I (the Torah) was a craftsman with him, and I was his delight every day' (Prov. 8:30). Thus whoever studies the Torah completes the world and preserves it. Further, God made the world through a breath, and through a breath it is preserved—the breath of those who assiduously study the Torah, and still more the breath of schoolchildren when reciting their lesson."

—Zohar Genesis 47a

One glorious chain of love, of giving and receiving unites all creatures.… None has power, or means, for itself; it receives in order to give; gives in order to receive, and finds therein the accomplishment of the purpose of its existence.

—Rabbi Samson Raphael Hirsch, "Letter 3," *Nineteen Letters*, pp. 29–30

Contacts with others invariably alter you, even if only a little. We are like chemicals: processed all day long and constantly compounded with other materials. One great, continuous process.

—Etty Hillesum, *An Interrupted Life*, p. 121

The good does not begin in the consciousness of man. It is being realized in the natural co-operation of all beings, in what they are for each other. Neither stars nor stones, neither atoms nor waves, but their belonging together, their interaction, the relation of all things to one another constitutes the universe. No cell could exist alone, all bodies are interdependent, affect and serve one another. Figuratively speaking, even rocks bear fruit, are full of unappreciated kindness, when their strength holds up a wall.

—Abraham Joshua Heschel, *Man Is Not Alone*, pp. 120–121

1. According to the Zohar, how are God and humanity partners in creating and sustaining the world? How does this compare with Rabbi Artson's view of relationship?

2. Where do you see Rabbi Samson Raphael Hirsch's chain of giving and receiving in the world around you?

3. Etty Hillesum uses the image of chemicals compounded with other chemicals. How does her metaphor relate to Process ideas?

4. "Even rocks bear fruit," says Abraham Joshua Heschel. How does this connect with the idea of co-creating?

Change, Choice, and Gift
The Dynamic Nature of Covenant

In this chapter, Rabbi Artson introduces the Process concept of "the lure" and how God exercises persuasive rather than coercive power. While the dominant Western view of God leaves us with a "bully in the sky" (p. 17), the Process view is that God works only within the laws of nature. Rabbi Artson shows that this conception from Process is in line with the rabbinic understanding that God acts within law and becomes vulnerable through entering into relationship with us.

Key Terms

- The lure
- Initial aim
- Prehension

Discussion Question

1. a) How does Process Thought's understanding of God's power differ from the dominant Western view?

   b) How do the rabbinic texts that Rabbi Artson quotes in this chapter relate to this Process view?

2. How do you react to this view of God? What disturbs you? What attracts you?

Text Study

> Now if you will obey Me and keep My covenant, you will be My treasure among all nations, for all the earth is Mine.
>
> —Exodus 19:5

> They shall make for Me a sanctuary and I will dwell inside them.
>
> —Exodus 25:8

You shall be holy to Me, for I, the Holy One, am holy, and I have set you apart from all other peoples that you should be Mine.

—Leviticus 20:26

See, a time is coming—declares the Holy One—when I will make a new covenant with the House of Israel and the House of Judah.... I will put My teaching into their innermost being and inscribe it upon their hearts. Then I will be their God, and they shall be My people. No longer will they need to teach one another, "Heed the Holy One"; for all of them, from the least of them to the greatest, shall heed Me—declares the Holy One.

—Jeremiah 31:31, 33–34

The Holy One, after issuing a decree, is the first to obey it, as it is stated "and they shall observe My observances, I am the Holy One" (Lev. 22:9). I am the one who was the first to observe the commandments of the Torah.

—Y. Rosh Ha-Shanah I:III

1. a) How do the first three quotations (all from the Torah) highlight the notion of a reciprocal relationship between God and the children of Israel?
   b) In what ways is this relationship shaped by our choices?

2. a) Jeremiah speaks of a renewed covenant that is found in our hearts. How does that compare to the idea of the lure?
   b) In this renewed relationship, the laws are found in everyone's core, not imposed from the outside. How does this intuitive sense of the Jewish imperative compare to the dominant theology of an outside, coercive God and to the Process idea of a permeating, persuasive God?

3. The passage from the Jerusalem Talmud portrays God as bound by the same laws as everything else in creation. How does that fit with the idea of an all-powerful external Deity? How does it fit with the idea of a pervasive and relational God?

Continuous Creation
Process Theology and the Metaphors of Our Origins

In this chapter, Rabbi Artson shows how Process Thought allows for pluralistic approaches when it comes to our understanding of creation. Starting with an acknowledgment of the limitations of human knowledge, Rabbi Artson demonstrates how an eternal cosmos co-existing with God is in line with biblical and rabbinic understandings of creation and is consistent with Process Thought as opposed to the dominant Western religious view of creation *ex nihilo*. However, Rabbi Artson is not definitive on this view and shows that two current scientific theories can be used to support both views. Rather than "asserting a false certainty," Artson sees both views as ultimately compatible with Process and classical Jewish thought.

Key Terms
- *Ex nihilo*

Discussion Questions
1. a) What does Rabbi Artson mean by saying that when it comes to the very large and the very small, "the only effective system of human relation and expression is the five M's: math, meditation, metaphor, music, and myth" (p. 22)?
   b) How does this relate to Rabbi Artson's aversion to "asserting a false certainty" (p. 28)?

2. a) What biblical and rabbinic texts support the concept of creation *ex nihilo*? The concept of an eternal universe?
   b) What scientific views support each of these concepts?
   c) How is Process compatible with both concepts?

3. What does it mean to say that "every moment *is* a moment of creation" (p. 24)?

Text Study

When God began to create heaven and earth—the earth being unformed and void, with darkness over the surface of the deep and a wind from God sweeping over the water—God said, "Let there be light"; and there was light. God saw that the light was good, and God separated the light from the darkness. God called the light Day, and the darkness He called Night. And there was evening and there was morning, a first day.

—Genesis 1:1–5

God renews every day the workings of Creation.

—Hagigah 12b

God created the world in a state of beginning. The universe is always in an uncompleted state, in the form of its beginning. It is not like a vessel at which the master works to finish it; it requires continuous labor and renewal by creative forces. Should these cease for only a second, the universe would return to primeval chaos.

—Reb Simha Bunam of Przysucha, *Siach Sarfei Kodesh* 2:17, in *The Hasidic Anthology*, edited by Louis I. Newman and Samuel Spitz, p. 61

Two and a half millennia of Western theology have made it easy to forget that throughout the ancient Near Eastern world, including Israel, the point of creation is not the production of matter out of nothing, but rather the emergence of a stable community in a benevolent and life-sustaining order.

—Jon D. Levenson, *Creation and the Persistence of Evil*, p. 12

1. According to the Genesis account, did God create everything out of nothing? What did God do that the Torah calls "creating"?

2. What does the Talmud mean when it says that God continually renews the work of creation?

3. Reb Simha Bunam was a great Hasidic master. How does his understanding of creation fit the model of *ex nihilo* (everything out of nothing in a single instant)? How does it fit the idea of creation as a continuous process? Which do you think is true?

4. Jon D. Levenson is a contemporary Hebrew Bible scholar. What do you make of his assertion? Is it what you understand Judaism to affirm? Should it be what Judaism affirms?

Life and the Experience of Evil
Process Theology's Eye-Opening Approach to Tension, Trauma, and Possibility

This chapter deals with the existence of evil and suffering in the world from a Process perspective. Drawing parallels to Maimonides's thoughts on the subject, Rabbi Artson argues that things we perceive as evil are either consequences of the dynamic nature of the world we live in or of the freedom humans have to ignore God's lure and make bad decisions that hurt others or ourselves. Rather than simply think about the causes of evil in the world, Process Thought invites us to "fight for justice, well-being, and compassion" (p. 34).

Discussion Questions

1. Rabbi Artson asserts that "the very source of dynamism and life" is also the source of "much of what we understand to be evil" (p. 31). How does that differ from the dominant theology? How do the dominant theology and Process Thought each view God's level of responsibility for evil?

2. Compare Maimonides's Aristotelian views on the nature of evil and suffering with Rabbi Artson's Process-inspired views on evil stemming from "three broad realities of life" (p. 32).

Text Study

> If the Holy One is with us, why has all this befallen us? Where are all His wondrous deeds about which our ancestors told us?
>
> —Gideon, in Judges 6:13

> You shall win, Holy One, if I make a claim against You, yet I shall present charges against You: Why does the way of the wicked prosper? Why are the workers of iniquity at ease?
>
> —Jeremiah 12:1

This ignoramus and those like him among the multitude consider that which exists only with reference to a human individual. Every ignoramus imagines that all that exists exists with a view to his individual sake; it is as if there were nothing that exists except him. And if something happens to him that is contrary to what he wishes, he makes the trenchant judgment that all that exists is an evil....

The first species of evil is that which befalls man because of the nature of coming-to-be and passing-away, I mean to say because of his being endowed with matter.... The evils of the second kind are those that men inflict upon one another, such as tyrannical domination of some of them over others.... The evils of the third kind are those that are inflicted upon any individual among us by his own action.... This kind is consequent upon all vices, I mean concupiscence for eating, drinking, and copulation, and doing these things with excess in regard to quantity or irregularly or when the quality of the foodstuffs is bad.

—Maimonides, *Guide of the Perplexed*, III:12

1. a) What motivates the speakers in the first two biblical quotations?

   b) Are these motivations surprising? Comforting?

2. a) Maimonides appeals for a shift in focus. How would you rephrase that shift based on our modern worldview? Why is this an important shift to achieve?

   b) How might a person's perspective change if he or she is no longer the center of the universe's concern? How does it challenge your own perspective?

3. Maimonides delineates three different kinds of suffering; for each kind, answer the following questions: How would the world look different if this type of suffering did not exist? Would that alternative be preferable to what we now have? Worse?

The Process of Revelation
Spiritual *and* Cognitive, Primal *and* Verbal

This chapter provides a Process understanding of revelation. Rabbi Artson begins by challenging three ways revelation can be understood based on the dominant metaphysics. The problems with these views of revelation stem from the assumption that God is essentially separate from the universe. Process, on the other hand asserts an integrated world where God and the cosmos are integrally connected. Thus there is no need to figure out how a radically different supernatural being can work inside of nature. God permeates all things and therefore anything within creation can be a source of revelation.

Rabbi Artson then moves on to discuss the particular nature of Jewish revelation. While revelation is universal to all people, it must be manifested in particularity for the universe to display true diversity and not simply conformity. Looking at the Jewish tradition through a Process lens, scripture is seen as "humanity verbalizing God's lure" (p. 47). This process of the Jewish community engaging with God did not stop with the canonization of any particular text in the tradition but continues even today.

Key Terms
- Universal revelation
- Special revelation
- Documentary hypothesis

Discussion Questions
1. a) What problems does the dominant metaphysics have when it comes to the concept of revelation?
   b) What are the possible solutions to these problems? How does Process Thought deal with these problems? (pp. 36–40)

2. What does Alfred North Whitehead mean when he says "religions commit suicide when they find their inspirations in their dogmas" (p. 39)?

3. a) How do the Psalms and medieval poems Rabbi Artson quotes in this chapter add to his argument? (pp. 41–42)

b) What phrases or images from the Psalms and poems are you most drawn to?

4. What is the relationship between universal revelation and special revelation? Why is special revelation necessary? (pp. 44–45)

5. a) How is Process Thought compatible with the documentary hypothesis?

   b) What does Rabbi Jakob Petuchowski mean when he says, "Literary history cannot solve the questions asked by Theology; and the question as to the *fact* of Revelation is a *theological* question" (p. 49)?

6. What does it mean to say that "receiving Torah is a process without end" (p. 49) and that "the Torah is meant to be the first word, not the last" (p. 51)? Why does Rabbi Artson distinguish these two points?

7. Why does a Process view of Torah insist that "ethics takes precedence"? How does the quotation from Isaiah 58 address this? (pp. 52–53)

Text Study

… a great voice that never stopped.

—Deuteronomy 5:19

My word is like fire—declares the Holy One—
and like a hammer that shatters rock!

—Jeremiah 23:29

Even what a sharp student will expound before a teacher has already been given to Moses at Sinai.

— Y. Pe'ah II:IV

Rav Judah said in the name of Rav, When Moses ascended on high he found the Holy One, blessed be He, engaged in affixing coronets to the letters. Said Moses, "Lord of the Universe, Who stays Your hand?" God answered, "There will arise a man, at the end of many generations, Akiva bar Yosef by name, who will expound upon each tittle heaps and heaps of laws." "Lord of the Universe," said Moses, "permit me to see him." God replied, "Turn around." Moses went and sat down behind eight rows [and listened to the discourses upon the law]. Not being able to follow their arguments he was ill at ease, but when they came to a certain subject and the disciples said to Rabbi Akiva, "From where do you know it?" and Rabbi Akiva replied, "It is a law given to Moses at Sinai," Moses was comforted. Thereupon he returned to the Holy Blessing One, and said, "Lord of the Universe, You have such a man and You give the Torah through me!" God replied, "Be silent, for such is My decree."

—Menahot 29b

It is clear that [while God's precepts to Israel are given] through words uttered in Torah, they are also given through words uttered by elders and sages.

> —Pesikta Rabbati, Piska 3

Each Jew must consider each and every moment as the one at which he is standing at Mount Sinai to receive the Torah. For people are subject to past and future, but with respect to the Blessing One there is no such distinction. And so each and every day God is giving the Torah to God's people Israel.

> —Abraham Joshua Heschel, *Oheiv Yisrael*, quoted in "Taking in the Torah of the Timeless Present," by Gordon Tucker, in *Jewish Mysticism and the Spiritual Life*, p. 67

It was possible that we heard from the mouth of the Holy Blessing One only the letter א of *anokhi*—that is, the first letter of the first word of the First Commandment.

> —Rebbe Naftali Tzvi Horowitz of Ropshitz, *Zera Kodesh* 2:40a, quoted in "Revelation at Sinai in the Hebrew Bible and in Jewish Theology," by Benjamin D. Sommer, in *The Journal of Religion*, p. 440

1. What does Deuteronomy mean when it claims that God's voice has never stopped? Does that sound "traditional" to you?

2. Jeremiah uses two dynamic images for Torah: fire and a rock-shattering hammer. Does that fit your personal view of revelation? Does it sound "traditional" to you?

3. a) The story of Moses in the classroom of Rabbi Akiva is often used to show the idea of a revelation that comes through Moses (and through Rabbi Akiva) but that grows through the new interpretations and teachings of each generation. Does that Talmud teaching fit a Process understanding (revelation as onging) or a dominant understanding (revelation as a one-time event)? Does it fit your understanding?

   b) What are some new understandings our generation has discovered in Torah?

4. Pesikta Rabbati acknowledges two pathways for revelation: words in Torah and the teachings of elders and sages. Are those the only two? Can you think of other sources?

5. a) If we are standing at Sinai at each and every moment, what is being asked of us?

   b) How does that expand our notion of Torah? Our notion of revelation?

Death and Afterlife
Two Paradigms of Hope and Enduring Significance

In this chapter, Rabbi Artson presents two possibilities when it comes to what happens after we die. Either human consciousness and identity ends at death and our energy patterns continue without any central organization, or "consciousness and identity continue unimpaired" (p. 59). Both are real possibilities within Process Thought and Rabbi Artson, as he mentioned in chapter 4, does not pretend to have certainty on this issue. He does maintain, however, that as we are patterns of energy now, so we will continue to be patterns of energy after we die.

Discussion Questions

1. a) How does Rabbi Artson keep the concept of an afterlife as a key requirement of Jewish belief while also avoiding "the false swagger of pretended certainty" (p. 57)?

   b) Do you agree that the concept of an afterlife is a key requirement of Jewish belief?

2. How is Process Thought consistent with both possibilities that Rabbi Artson lays out regarding what happens after we die? (p. 59)

Text Study

> The dead cannot praise the Lord, nor can any who go down into silence. But we will bless the Lord from this time forth and for evermore. Hallelujah!
>
> —Psalm 115:17–18

> "O mortal, can these bones live again?" I replied, "O the Holy One God, only You know." And God said to me, "Prophesy over these bones and say to them: O dry bones, hear the word of the Holy One! Thus says the Holy One God to these bones: I will cause breath to enter you and you shall live again."
>
> —Ezekiel 37:3–5

From Sheol itself I will save them,
Redeem them from very death.
Where, O death, are your plagues?
Your pestilence where, O Sheol?

   —Hosea 13:14

This world is not like the Coming World.

   —Ketubot 111b

The goodness of the coming world—people don't have the power to explain or articulate it, and can't know its greatness, beauty, or essence, because it doesn't have dimension or likeness or image.

   —Tanhuma, Va-Yikra 8

"A song, a hymn for the Sabbath day" (Ps. 92:1). A song, a hymn for the future, for a day that is entirely a Shabbat, and rest for everlasting life.

   —Tamid 33b

The Sages did not use the expression "the world to come" with the intention of implying that this realm does not exist at present or that the present realm will be destroyed and then that realm will come into being. The matter is not so. Rather, the world to come exists and is present. It is only called the world to come because that life comes to a man after life in this world in which we exist, as souls clothed in bodies. This realm of existence is presented to all men at first.

   —Maimonides, Hilkhot Teshuvah, *Mishneh Torah* 8:8

1. a) Based on the three biblical verses, can you determine what is the biblical view of an afterlife? Is there more than one possible view?

    b) What message is the Bible trying to convey to us?

2. The quotations from Ketubot and Tanhuma indicate that there is no possible way for a living human to accurately know or conceive of what the afterlife is like—yet we affirm its existence. What is the value of an affirmation we hold but can't describe or define? Can you think of other such foundational affirmations in your life?

3. Tamid uses the metaphor of an eternal Shabbat to convey a sense of the afterlife. Does that image work for you? Can you think of other images that might also help convey a sense of the afterlife?

4. a) Maimonides insists that eternity isn't waiting in some subsequent chronological sense, but is available at all moments if we are but aware of it. What might we do to raise our consciousness of eternity more often?

    b) Would that be a useful practice? How might that affect day-to-day life?

The Power of Resilient Love
The Persuasive Persistence of Loving-Kindness

In part 2 of God of Becoming and Relationship, *Rabbi Artson moves on from the foundational ideas* of Process Theology to argue that "much of Judaism is, in fact, inherently Process" (p. 61). Rabbi Artson begins this section with a discussion of the Jewish understanding of covenantal love, or *chesed*, which he insists must be placed at the core of Judaism. Rabbi Artson presents the Jewish understanding of love as a persistent and dynamic relationship that integrates our internal emotions with our external actions, manifesting itself in justice (*tzedek*), peace (*shalom*), and blessing or well-being (*berakhah*).

Key Terms

- *Chesed*
- *Ahavah*
- *Tzedek*
- *Shalom*
- *Berakhah*

Discussion Questions

1. What distinction does Rabbi Artson draw between *chesed* and *ahavah*? How does his understanding of *chesed* fit into his larger Process Theology? (p. 66)

2. Rabbi Artson translates *olam chesed yibaneh* from Psalm 89:3 as "I will build this world with love." Compare this to the NJPS translation: "Your steadfast love is confirmed forever." What do these different translations each imply about the nature of God's love?

3. How do the two stories of the Sassover Rebbe fit in with Rabbi Artson's larger understanding of the nature of love in the Jewish tradition? (pp. 67–68)

4. How is covenantal love different from both popular culture's understanding of love and the misunderstanding of covenantal love as "an objective assessment of priorities" (p. 70)?

5. What is the relationship between covenantal love and justice (*tzedek*), peace (*shalom*), and blessing or well-being (*berakhah*)? (pp. 71–72)

Text Study

And now, O Israel, what does the Holy One your God demand of you? Only this: to revere the Holy One your God, to walk only in God's paths, to love God, and to serve the Holy One your God with all your heart and soul, keeping the Holy One's commandments and laws, which I enjoin upon you today, for your good. Mark, the heavens to their uttermost reaches belong to the Holy One your God, the earth and all that is on it! Yet it was to your ancestors that the Holy One was drawn in love for them, so that God chose you, their lineal descendants, from among all peoples—as is now the case. Cut away, therefore, the thickening about your hearts and stiffen your necks no more. For the Holy One your God is God supreme and Holy One supreme, the great, the mighty, and the awesome God, who shows no favor and takes no bribe, but upholds the cause of the orphan and the widow, and befriends the stranger, providing food and clothing. You too must befriend the stranger, for you were strangers in the land of Egypt.

—Deuteronomy 10:12–19

1. What does this passage say about our love for God and God's love for the Jewish people? What is the nature of our relationship with God in these verses?

2. a) What is the connection between the love of God and acting justly towards others?

   b) Have you experienced this connection in your own life?

3. The passage starts with theology and metaphysics and ends with ethics. In what way does this parallel Judaism itself?

"The Body Is the Glory of the Soul"
Finding Holiness in the Integration of Spirited Bodies

In this chapter, Rabbi Artson challenges the dichotomy between the spiritual and the physical, a split that goes "to the very core of Western civilization" (p. 74) and results in the elevation of the spiritual over the physical. Rabbi Artson argues that this dichotomy is a false one and presents an alternative idea from Process Theology: the spiritual as a process that is inherently manifested through physical bodies.

Rabbi Artson concludes this chapter by insisting that this Process view is more in line with the classical rabbinic sources, which, only moderately influenced by Plato, see that "body and soul are interlocking aspects of a fully mature human entity and that both of them are necessary vehicles for holiness and godliness in the world" (p. 78).

Discussion Questions

1. a) What insights does Rabbi Artson see the mind-body dichotomy presenting Judaism? (pp. 76–77)
    b) What limitations in this view lead to Rabbi Artson ultimately rejecting it? (pp. 77–78) How might we be able to keep these insights without the limitations?

2. a) How do the sources Rabbi Artson cites from Ta'anit and Eruvin view the body?
    b) How would our religious lives be different "if we trained ourselves to value the holiness of our intestines" (p. 79)?

3. How do issues of gender and human dignity appear in the light of the dominant dichotomy as opposed to how they might look in a more integrated approach? (p. 79)

4. How does an integrated view of the body and spirit lead to a call to action in the world? (p. 80)

Text Study

Praised are you, Holy One our God, Majesty of space-time, who with wisdom fashioned the human body, creating openings, arteries, glands, and organs, marvelous in structure, intricate in design. Should but one of them, by being blocked or opened, fail to function, it would be impossible to exist. Praised are you, Holy One, healer of all flesh who sustains our bodies in wondrous ways.

The soul which You, my God, have given me is pure. You created it. You formed it, You breathed it into me; You keep body and soul together. One day You will take my soul from me, to restore it to me in life eternal. So long as this soul is within me I acknowledge You, Lord my God, my ancestors' God, Master of all creation, sovereign of all souls. Praised are You, Holy One, who restores the soul to the lifeless, exhausted body.

—Birkhot Ha-Shachar, in *Siddur Sim Shalom*, edited with translations by Jules Harlow, pp. 9–11

"The breath of life" (Gen. 2:7). It is called by five names: *nefesh, ruach, neshamah, yechidah, chayah*. The *nefesh* is the blood, as it is written, "the blood is the nefesh" (Deut. 12:23). *Ruach*, because it ascends and descends, as it says, "who knows if the ruah of people ascends" (Eccl. 3:21)? *Neshamah* is the countenance, as one would say, "a good countenance." *Chayah*, for all the limbs die and yet it lives (*chayah*). *Yechidah*, for all of the limbs are duplicated and it remains unique.

—Genesis Rabbah 14:9

1. a) Do you think the two prayers from Birkhot Ha-Shachar, said during the morning service, fit more with the dominant Western mind-body dichotomy or with Rabbi Artson's Process model? Why?

   b) If you think they are closer to the dominant Western view, is there a way to reimagine these prayers through a Process lens?

2. a) In the *Siddur*, the prayer for the study of Torah is traditionally placed between these two prayers. What do you think the authors of the *Siddur* had in mind when they organized the morning service in this way?

   b) What insights from Process Theology may help to explain this order?

3. The Midrash above is quite ancient. It uses all the Hebrew terms we associate with a soul but seems to mean something very different than the Platonized disembodied spiritual substance. How might a more authentic and bodily sense of *nefesh* and *neshamah* change how you read the two prayers above? Does this new reading better fit a Process approach?

The Thresholds of Our Lives
Judaism's Rituals and Observances of Becoming

This chapter turns its attention to Jewish life-cycle occasions and how they support the Process Thought idea that "we aren't human *beings*, so much as human *becomings*" (p. 82). Jewish rituals provide a means for us to navigate through the stages of our lives as well as challenge the dominant cultural perception "that life belongs to each solitary individual … and that our living links us only externally with other objects—human or otherwise—in the world" (p. 85). In contrast to this "constricted, brutal, and isolating" worldview, Jewish life-cycle rituals demonstrate the truths found in Process Thought—that we are integrally connected to each other, God, and all creation.

Key Terms
- Liminal

Discussion Questions

1. a) Why are liminal spaces and times particularly significant to us?
   b) How do Jewish rituals deal with these moments of liminality?
   c) What does Process Thought add to our understanding of liminality?

2. How does Rabbi Artson's view of the life cycle contrast with the "dominant cultural perception that life belongs to each solitary individual" (p. 85)?

3. In this chapter, Rabbi Artson quotes Mishnah Avot 2:4: "Do God's will as though it were yours, so that God will do your will as though it were God's. Nullify your will for God's, that God may nullify the will of others for yours" (p. 86). How does this quotation relate to the celebration of life-cycle events?

4. Each of the celebrated moments of the life cycle also marks significant advances for the covenant between God and the Jewish people. How does the Process understanding of relationship as dynamic and shifting help us see those living qualities in rituals of birth, adulthood, marriage, and death? (pp. 87–88)

Text Study

The creation of a child is like the creation of the world.

  —Tanhuma, Pekudei 3

Just as the womb takes in and sends forth, so the grave takes in and sends forth.

  —Sanhedrin 92a

When the Holy Blessing One revealed Himself at the Sea, the children recognized God first, as it says: "This is my God, and I will beautify God" (Exod. 15:2).

  —Sotah 11b

Rabbi Yochanan would stand in deference to an aged gentile, explaining: "How many experiences has he gone through!"

  —Kiddushin 33a

One who learned Torah as a youth should learn Torah in old age. One who had disciples as a youth should have disciples in old age, as it says: "in the morning, sow your seed" (Eccl. 11:6).

  —Yevamot 62b

Do not separate yourself from the community!

  —Hillel, Mishnah Avot 2:5

By virtue of human nature, people seek to form communities.

  —Maimonides, *Guide of the Perplexed*, III:49

1. a) In dominant theology, how might you compare the creation of a child to the creation of the world?
    b) In Process Thought, what about the idea of creation changes and what gets added?

2. a) The Talmud describes birth and death in Process terms (as a process of giving and receiving). How does this help us frame the liminal moments in life?
    b) Are there any moments that are not liminal? Are there any moments that are not in relationship (taking in and giving forth)?

3. a) Why would it be that children might be the first to recognize God in novel situations?
    b) What does that say about the proper role of imagination, fantasy, and play for a rich religious life? For a fully engaged life?
    c) How can adults reclaim these gifts?

4. a) What would the world look like if each time we saw an elderly person, we considered how many, and how varied, their experiences must have been? And what if we considered all that we could learn from their experiences?

b) Could we extend that to younger people? Different ethnicities or religions than our own? Different orientations or regions than our own?

c) Our own life would become richer if we could integrate all these many ways of being human into it. How might we do that? What might that look like?

d) How can literature, drama, and art play a role in our internalizing of other people's vastly different experiences? What are some examples of this in your own life?

5. What is the value of learning material in maturity that we've already learned in our youths?

6. a) If we are who we are because of our relationships to others, what does that imply about the role of communities?

b) How does being part of a circle of communities shape you?

Imperatives of a Loving Heart
Responding to Life's Lure through Sacred Commandments

This chapter presents a Process understanding of mitzvot *and* halakhah: *a view "that we and the world are invited to greater engagement, relationship, compassion, and justice" (p. 90). This view is an alternative to both the "hyperliteral notion of a tyrant who literally throws the book at us and ... a vast meaningless universe" (p. 90). Rabbi Artson also challenges the popular notion that there is a strict dichotomy between thought and action in Judaism, suggesting instead that each is a phase in "an unending feedback loop" where thoughts and actions express and modify each other (p. 92). It is the interplay between thought and action that provides Judaism its vitality. While each* mitzvah *is an individual sacred deed, the* halakhah *is the systematic attempt of the Rabbis to "translate God's love and justice into the fabric of Jewish living" (p. 95), and provides the larger context for the* mitzvot. *In conclusion, Rabbi Artson proposes that we understand the nature of* mitzvah *not as a command performed because of fear, but rather because of love; that we see God not as a "Sovereign in the sky, rewarding and punishing," but rather as a "Parent, Teacher, Lover, Spouse, [or] Covenant Partner" (p. 99).*

Key Terms
- Panpsychism

Discussion Questions
1. What does Rabbi Artson mean when he says "the commandedness of the *mitzvot* comes from within" (p. 91)?

2. a) Rabbi Artson maintains that Jewish observance is neither "a system of distilled ideas" nor "a code of behavioral ideals" (p. 93). What are the strengths and weaknesses of these two ways of viewing Jewish observance?

   b) How does a Process view address the weaknesses?

3. a) Rabbi Artson rhetorically asks, "Why not just speak of *mitzvot* without reference to *halakhah* at all?" (p. 95). What would it look like to separate the *mitzvot* from the *halakhah*?

   b) What are some reasons we might want to do this? Why does Rabbi
      Artson ultimately find those reasons not compelling?

4. According to Maimonides and the Maggid Mishneh, why should we
   observe the *mitzvot*? How does this compare with Rabbi Artson's Process
   Theology?

5. How does the Aramaic word צוותא (*tzavta*) help us better understand the
   concept of *mitzvot* (pp. 97–98)?

6. In this chapter, Rabbi Artson uses many different metaphors to describe
   mitzvot and *halakhah* (the relationship of mind and body, a tree, the act of
   walking). Which metaphor do you find most compelling? Why?

Text Study

> You shall keep My laws and My rules, by the pursuit of which a person shall
> live: I am the Holy One.
>
> > —Leviticus 18:5

> I am the Holy One who freed you from the land of Egypt. You shall faithfully
> observe all My laws and all My rules: I am the Holy One.
>
> > —Leviticus 19:36–37

> You shall sanctify yourselves and be holy, for I the Holy One am your God.
> You shall faithfully observe My laws; I the Holy One make you holy.
>
> > —Leviticus 20:7–8

> Keep them therefore and do them, for this is your wisdom and your under-
> standing in the sight of the nations, who shall hear all these statutes, and
> say, Surely this great nation is a wise and understanding people.
>
> > —Deuteronomy 4:6

> Every commandment from among these 613 commandments exists either
> with a view to communicating a correct opinion, or to putting an end to an
> unhealthy opinion, or to communicating a rule of justice, or to warding off an
> injustice, or to endowing men with a noble moral quality, or warning them
> against an evil moral quality. Thus all [the commandments] are bound up
> with three things: opinions, moral qualities, and political civic actions.
>
> > —Maimonides, *Guide of the Perplexed*, III:31

> In this immediacy, we may not "express" God, but rather address God in the
> individual commandment.
>
> > —Franz Rosenzweig, *On Jewish Learning*, p. 122

1. a) The passages from Leviticus offer three benefits of or rationales for the *mitzvot* that have nothing to do with authority or coercive power. What are those three?*

    b) How would a Process understanding of dynamism and relational identity articulate that biblical perspective?

2. a) According to the passage in Deuteronomy, the sign of getting the *mitzvot* right is that a well-meaning Gentile will see us practice them and judge them to be wise. How would using that criterion to measure authentic observance change Jewish religion today? How would it change Jewish culture?

    b) How would a Process perspective explain the need for that criterion?

3. a) Maimonides offers three purposes for the *mitzvot*: correct opinion, lofty morals, and social equity and justice. How do those goals fit with the dominant theology's understanding of *mitzvot* and *halakhah*?

    b) How do they fit with a Process understanding of *mitzvot* and *halakhah*?

    c) Which fits better with your own views?

4. a) Franz Rosenzweig insists that we should focus not on defining God, but relaing directly; not on speaking about God, but speaking to God. He sees the *mitzvot* as our way of addressing God. Does that make sense to you?

    b) What are the verbal ways we can address God? Non-verbal ways?

Teacher's tip: Enhancing life, affirming freedom, celebrating holiness.

Revelation and a Living Relationship of Love
An Open-Ended Torah and Building Holy Community

In this chapter, Rabbi Artson turns his attention to Process Theology's conception of revelation. Contrary to the dominant view of revelation as a one-time event with God delivering an unchanging Torah to a passive humanity, Process sees revelation as "ongoing, relational, dynamic, and continuous" (p. 101). Torah represents, for Rabbi Artson, "the response of the Jews to a heightened experience of God" (p. 102). As such, we are partners in this continuous revelation that is inseparably human and divine. This means that the authority of Torah is not coercive, but persuasive. This also means that as Jews we both choose and are chosen, "although most emphatically not because of intrinsic superiority.... We choose/are chosen because God is discerned in our relationship" (pp. 105–106).

Key Terms

- Inferior *yirah*
- Superior *yirah*

Discussion Questions

1. Rabbi Artson opens this chapter with an image of a book being brought down to Moses from a descending arm, an image he calls "an accurate pictorial presentation of the dominant view of revelation as shaped by much of medieval philosophy" (p. 101). What pictorial representations might be more appropriate for a Process understanding of revelation?

2. a) In the midrash that Rabbi Artson quotes from Shabbat 88a, the rabbis conclude that since the revelation at Sinai was coercive, it is not binding. What implications does this view have for our understanding of the Torah today?

   b) How does the Jewish people's voluntary acceptance of the Torah during the time of Mordecai and Esther shape our relationship with Torah? (pp. 103–104)

3. How does Process Thought address the either/or dichotomy that "either the Jews are chosen, hence superior, or all peoples are equal and none are chosen" (p. 104)?

Text Study

For I have singled him out, that he may instruct his children and his posterity to keep the way of the Holy One by doing what is just and right.

—Genesis 18:19

All the nations of the earth shall bless themselves by your descendants, because you have obeyed My command.

—Genesis 22:18

Your descendants shall be as the dust of the earth; you shall spread out to the west and to the east, to the north and to the south. All the families of the earth shall bless themselves by you and your descendants.

—Genesis 28:14

For you are a people consecrated to the Holy One your God: of all the peoples on earth the Holy One your God chose you to be God's treasured people. It is not because you are the most numerous of peoples that the Holy One set His heart on you and chose you—indeed, you are the smallest of peoples; but it was because the Holy One favored you and kept the oath God made to your ancestors that the Holy One freed you with a mighty hand and rescued you from the house of bondage, from the power of Pharaoh king of Egypt.

—Deuteronomy 7:6–8

Yet the matter remains unclear, since we do not know whether the Holy Blessing One chose Jacob or whether Jacob chose the Holy Blessing One.

—Sifrei Deuteronomy, Piska 312

Revelation is not a one-way directive from above or a human projection from below. Revelation is the dialogue of reciprocal covenant, an ongoing process of listening and interpreting, of receiving and giving.

—Rabbi Harold Schulweis, *For Those Who Can't Believe*, p. 87

1. a) According to the first quotation from Genesis, revelation happens one person at a time; is transmitted from parent to child or teacher to disciple; and is for the sake of learning to do what is right and just. How does this vision of revelation feel different than verbal revelation on a single occasion?

    b) How does this version of revelation show up in your life? Your family? Your community?

2. a) The second two Genesis passages speak of the nations of the world blessing themselves through us because of how we live Torah and serve as role models. This suggests that, while Jews have a distinctive role, the Torah is intended to benefit all humanity. Does this integration of particular and universal seem right to you?

   b) How would you expound this idea using Process vocabulary?

3. a) The passage from Deuteronomy uses a shocking image: God chose the Jews because God fell in love with us (and not because of any objective merits we possess). What does this view say about the relationship element of revelation and chosenness? Can God fall in love with other peoples or groups too?

   b) What would that pluralistic model of love relationships imply about the value of distinctive religious paths? About their ability to learn from each other?

4. a) The Midrash causes confusion—we don't really know whether it was God who chose Israel or Israel who chose God. Does it matter? Could it be both?

   b) How does this relationship model shift our understanding of revelation in our day?

5. a) Rabbi Schulweis speaks of revelation as a dialogue, a continuing process of listening and interpreting. Does that understanding correspond to your own?

   b) Does it fit the practices of your community?

   c) Does it make distinctive demands on us? What is our job in that view of revelation?

Everywhere I Go
Process Theology's Embrace of Israel *and* Diaspora

Rabbi Artson discussed the mind-body and thought-action dichotomies in earlier chapters; here he tackles the Israel-Diaspora dichotomy. Once again, Rabbi Artson uses the Process concept of dipolarity to argue for a middle path between either seeing Israel as the only place worthy of our allegiance or as a place that is no different than any other. Combating these "simplistic distortions" (p. 108), Rabbi Artson creates a more nuanced picture by bringing a number of classical Jewish texts that both maintain the importance (indeed, necessity) of the Diaspora as well as extoll the uniqueness of Israel.

Discussion Questions

1. a) In what ways do the classical sources that Rabbi Artson quotes show that Diaspora is to be seen "not as a curse but as a promise" (p. 109)?

   b) What are the benefits of Diaspora? What are the challenges?

2. a) Rabbi Artson states, "We do not necessarily take the Bible literally, but we do take the Bible seriously" (p. 114). What does this statement mean in regards to the particularity of the Land of Israel?

   b) What are other consequences of taking the Bible seriously but not literally?

3. According to Rabbi Artson, what allows the Rabbis to maintain that nine-tenths of the world's wisdom and beauty are to be found in Israel? (pp. 114–115)

4. What would our lives look like if we took Rabbi Artson's advice to "muster the courage to transcend *either/or* and to embrace the heady virtue of dipolarity" (p. 119)?

Text Study

> If you remain in this land [Bavel], I will build you and not overthrow, I will plant you and not uproot; for I regret the punishment I have brought upon you.
>
> —Jeremiah 42:10

The remnant of Jacob shall be,
In the midst of the many peoples,
Like dew from the Holy One,
Like droplets on grass—
Which do not look to any [person]
Nor place their hope in mortals.

> —Micah 5:6

Assuredly, a time is coming—declares the Holy One—when it shall no more be said, "As the Holy One lives who brought the Israelites out of the land of Egypt," but rather, "As the Holy One lives who brought the Israelites out of the northland, and out of all the lands to which God had banished them." For I will bring them back to their land, which I gave to their ancestors.

> —Jeremiah 16:14–15

Study with all your heart and with all your soul to know My ways and to watch at the doors of My Torah. Keep My Torah in your heart and let My fear be before your eyes. Keep your mouth from all sin and purify and sanctify yourself from all transgression and iniquity, and I will be with you in every place.

> —Berakhot 17a

The ingathering of the exiles is as great as the day when heaven and earth were created.

> —Pesahim 88a

1. The first two quotations seem to suggest that there is a constructive value to Jews living across the globe, rather than all remaining in the Land of Israel. What are the positive virtues of the Jewish Diaspora for Jewish culture, survival, and religion, and also for human advancement in general? What are the challenges of the Jewish Diaspora?

2. The next quotation, from Jeremiah, seems to indicate that our return to our homeland, the Land of Israel, is the fulfillment of God's plan and promise, something wonderful that is to be celebrated. What are the positive virtues of the Jewish return to our homeland, both for Jewish culture, survival, and religion? What are the challenges of this ingathering?

3. a) What do you make of the extensive quotations extolling and condemning the *galut* (Diaspora) *and* extensive traditional quotations extolling and condemning the return to the Land of Israel?

   b) Is there a way to integrate these positions?

4. Where do you stand on this issue? Was it ever a real conversation about where your family was going to settle and stay?

5. What are your connections to the Land, State, and people of Israel? How do you stay connected?

The Process of Offering Ourselves
What We Do When We Pray

This chapter presents an understanding of what prayer is from a Process Theology perspective. Prayer is not to be seen as a magical request for God to break the rules of nature, but rather as an act to "re-center ourselves with God at the core" (p. 125). Prayer is the act that allows us to better hear God's divine lure, guiding us to take the best next step in our lives. Prayer can be spontaneous or scripted. In fact, both types of prayer are in symbiotic relationship, with each one reinforcing the other. While realizing the limits of intercessory prayer, Rabbi Artson maintains that praying for other people to recover from illness is worthwhile as a way to "raise to explicit consciousness the vague concern for the other" (p. 128).

Key Terms

- *Davar*
- *Kavanah**

Discussion Questions

1. What are some problems with prayer that result from the dominant theology's view of God? (pp. 123–124)

2. How does prayer fit into the Process idea that "God works with, in, and through creation as it is" (p. 125)?

3. What does it mean to see liturgical prayer as similar to reading a script? (pp. 126–127)

4. From the perspective of Process Theology, in what ways does intercessory prayer work? In what ways does intercessory prayer not work?

*Teacher's tip: Although the term is not explicitly mentioned in this chapter, it may be useful to introduce the concept of keva *along with* kavanah.

Text Study

In the evening, morning, and afternoon I will speak and cry aloud and God will hear my voice.

—Psalm 55:18

Cast your eyes downward as though looking at the ground and your heart upward as though standing in heaven.

—Yevamot 105b

See yourself in prayer as though God were facing you, as it is stated, "I have set God before me always" (Ps. 16:8).

—Sanhedrin 22a

Prayer is union with the Divine Presence. Just as two people will move their bodies back and forth as they begin the act of love, so must a person accompany the beginning of prayer with the rhythmic swaying of the body. But as one reaches the heights of union with the Presence, the movement of the body ceases.

—Zava'at Ha-Rivash 7b

Do not think that the words of prayer as you say them go up to God. It is not the words themselves that ascend; it is rather the burning desire of your heart that rises like smoke toward Heaven. If your prayer consists only of words and letters, and does not contain your heart's desire—how can it rise up to God?

—Or Ha-Meir 3:16c

Our prayers are answered not when we are given what we ask, but when we are challenged to be what we can be.

—Rabbi Morris Adler, quoted in "You Believe What!? Theology, Belief, Faith and Religion" by Joe Klein

1. Psalms combines a sense of regular times for prayer (three times per day) with a sense of spontaneous speech and cries. Is there a tension between fixed prayer and spontaneous prayer? If so, how do you resolve that tension? How would a Process approach deal with it?
2. a) Yevamot tells us to pray with our eyes downward and heart upward—another tension. How can we integrate these seemingly opposite directions of the soul in our prayers?
   b) What does this instruction try to teach us? Is this a form of dipolarity?
3. a) The Talmud in Sanhedrin underscores prayer as relationship, seeing God as though before us. Notice the "as though." If God is not really before us, what is the Talmud hinting at?
   b) How does prayer as relationship help? Could it hinder?

4. The Hasidic source Ziva'at Ha-Rivash goes even further with the idea of prayer as relationship, comparing it to the eros of making love: lots of motion at the beginning, complete stillness after the completion. Does this image make prayer more appealing or less? More accessible or less? Can you imagine praying as an act of lovemaking?

5. a) If prayer isn't the words, but is instead the burning desire of the heart, then why all those words in the *Siddur*? Are they helpful to the ascent of our hearts, or are they hindrances?

    b) How could a Process understanding of what prayer is help with the challenge of praying with other people's words?

God Is Becoming
Tragedy, Judaism, and Process

This chapter focuses on the subject of suffering and tragedy in our lives and how Process Thought can "offer a haven for those needing consolation, and a light of honesty and truth so our healing would be real" (p. 130). Process Thought maintains that we, and all of creation, are co-creators with God. We have true freedom to make choices and therefore God is "vulnerable to surprise and disappointment" (p. 131). Furthermore, God does not suspend the laws of nature through which the universe unfolds. This is a contrast to the dominant view, which sees God's power as coercive, leaving us to feel betrayed when tragedy strikes our lives. Instead, Process Thought allows us to see God "in the steady constant lure toward good choices and responsibility" (p. 132).

Discussion Questions

1. Rabbi Artson makes a distinction between the way we generally perceive the world as being composed of objects and the Process concept of reality as becoming. How does this distinction fit into this chapter's larger theme of tragedies in our lives?

2. What are the problems with responding to tragedy by saying, "It's a mystery," or, "We can't understand"? What alternative does Process Thought provide?

3. This chapter has a pastoral context—responding to the tragedy of a particular student's death. Is responding to tragedy ever theoretical? Does recognizing its pastoral function change how we might try to address the issue of human suffering?

Text Study

It was taught: Rabbi Yakov said: "There is not a *mitzvah* written in the Torah whose reward is mentioned next to it which is not dependent on the resurrection of the dead. Concerning honoring your father and mother it is written, 'that you may long endure, and that you may fare well' (Deut. 5:16). Concerning sending away the mother bird from the nest it is written, 'in order that that you may fare well and have a long life' (Deut. 22:7). Now, if a father said to his son, 'Go up to the loft and bring me the chicks,' and he went up to the loft, sent away the mother and took the young, and on his return he fell and died, where is his 'faring well' and where is his 'long life'? But 'in order that you may fare well,' means on the day that is completely fare [the World to Come]; and 'that you may long endure,' means on the day that is completely long [the World to Come]."

Perhaps this never happened? Rabbi Yakov saw it happen. Or perhaps the son was considering sinning? The Holy Blessing One does not combine an evil thought with an act. Or perhaps he was considering idolatry, and it is written, "I will hold the House of Israel to account for their thoughts" (Ezek. 14:5)? This too was like what Rabbi Yakov said—"if you should think that mitzvot are rewarded in this world, why did these mitzvot not protect him from such thoughts?"

Rabbi Eleazar said, "Those who are doing a mitzvah are never harmed." Perhaps when they are going to perform the mitzvah it is different [from returning from fulfilling a *mitzvah*, when one might be harmed]? But Rabbi Eleazar said, "Those who are doing a *mitzvah* are never harmed, either when going or returning."

Rather it was a damaged ladder, so injury was likely, and whenever injury is likely one must not depend on a miracle, for it is written, "and Samuel replied 'How can I go? If Saul hears of it, he will kill me'" (1 Sam. 14:2).

—Kiddushin 39b

1. a) What is the problem inherent in the story of the father sending his son up to bring back the chicks? What is Rabbi Yakov's solution to this problem?

   b) How does his solution compare with a Process understanding of tragedy and suffering?

2. a) The Talmud seems to be very uncomfortable with this story and offers several possible explanations to make it less problematic. How do each of these solutions attempt to solve the problem? How do they fail? In the end, what explanation holds up?

   b) Based on this explanation, who is ultimately responsible for the boy's untimely death? How does this solution compare to a Process understanding of tragedy and suffering?

3. How does this story resonate with you in your life and your own personal experiences of tragedy? Is it comforting? Challenging?

Ever Dying, Never Dead
Finding Gifts in Our Mortality

In this chapter, Rabbi Artson turns his attention to our mortality. He maintains that since we are aware of our own mortality, "we humans live as dying creatures" (p. 135). It is this awareness that allows us to realize what is important and inspires us to live fully. Rabbi Artson concludes by stating that even those who have come before us are still present in our lives, if not physically. This further inspires us to make the most of each moment we have, using the fact that we are "eternally dying" to teach us to live.

Key Terms

- Objective immortality
- Subjective immortality

Discussion Questions

1. What are your personal beliefs about dying, death, and the afterlife? Do you think these beliefs shape the way you currently live your life? How?

2. How do you understand the teachings of Jewish tradition on this topic? Do you find these assertions plausible? Helpful?

3. Rabbi Artson begins this chapter with a discussion of the *kittel*, a garment worn at one's wedding, during the Passover Seder, during Yom Kippur, and as a funeral shroud. What is the connection between each of these events and how does that fit into the larger theme of this chapter?

4. a) What does it mean to believe in the "eternal coming of the Messiah" (p. 136)?

   b) How does it relate to Rabbi Artson's assertion that we are "eternally dying" (p. 139)?

Text Study

Rabbi Artson invites us to make this pledge in the light of our own mortality:

> This time is no longer my time. It is my gift to God. And I will live my life in such a way that every moment is my gift to God. The way I treat the people I love and those I do not love, I will offer up as a gift. The way I work to build community, I offer, God, this gift to You. The way I work to strengthen Judaism and the Jewish people, a sense of the family of humanity, the way I represent my love for Israel and for Zion—everywhere I do these, God, I give to you. The way I care for Your creation and walk lightly on Your beautiful blue-green planet, this, God, I give to You as my gift. My remaining hours, I give to You. (pp. 138–139)

1. What do you see as the purpose of making such a pledge? What do you see as the purpose of viewing your remaining time on earth as a gift belonging to God?

2. Would such a pledge change the way you use your remaining time? How would it improve your life or burden it?

3. If you were writing your own pledge, what would it say?

Untrammeled Future
Freedom and Becoming

In this chapter, Rabbi Artson introduces the Process idea that everything in the universe has "an appropriate capacity to make choices that shape our futures" (p. 140). Our own self-agency is considerable, even as it is limited by our own past choices as well as the choices of everything around us. This contrasts with a deterministic view where everything is merely the mechanistic outcome of everything that came before. Process, however, sees the universe constantly moving towards novelty, with God acting as the lure in the universe. We are free to accept or deny the divine lure, which is both the good news and the bad news that comes with freedom.

Key Terms

- Determinism
- Agency; self-agency
- Freedom

Discussion Questions

1. Why do many philosophers and scientists insist that freedom is delusional?

2. Does the world feel deterministic to you, or do you feel like you have freedom to make your own choices?

3. a) What is the case to be made for an open future and for creaturely freedom?

   b) Do you find this argument persuasive? Why or why not?

4. Do you think the fact that the philosophers and scientists who hold that the universe is deterministic "live as though they are free to decide their own futures" (p. 143) is a satisfactory refutation of determinism?

Text Study

All is foreseen, yet freedom of choice is given.

—Rabbi Akiva, Mishnah Avot 3:19

The Creator (Who is exalted) does not allow His power to interfere in the least with the actions of men, nor does He compel them to be either obedient or disobedient.

—Rav Saadia Gaon, *Sefer Emunot Ve-De'ot*, chapter 4

The reasonable way, in my opinion, is for man to beware of placing himself in a position that he may be compelled to regret. Although men have not the power so to control themselves that they can choose all their qualities, nevertheless they can desire to rise gradually from a base to a lofty course, and from faulty qualities to sound ones. The acme of bliss for man is to be able to bridle his soul, to rule it, to lead it along the right way. He whose nature yields to his intellect becomes lordly; his merit becomes high and profitable, and his deeds are praised.

—Solomon ibn Gabirol, *Tikkun Middot Ha-Nefesh* 83

A person cannot know God if he does not know his own spirit, soul, and body. For of what use is a person's wisdom to him if he does not know the makeup of his soul?

—Rabbi Abraham ibn Ezra, *Sefer Ha-Yashar*, Exodus 31:18

When a person weighs their actions constantly and directs them toward their midpoints, they will be on the most elevated human plane possible. They will thereby approach God and grasp God's will. This is the most perfect path in the service of God.

—Maimonides, *Shemonah Perakim* 4

What I'm really interested in is whether God could have made the world in a different way; that is, whether the necessity of logical simplicity leaves any freedom at all.

—Albert Einstein, quoted in *The Scientific Imagination: Case Studies*, by Gerald Holton, p. xii

1. Rabbi Akiva seems to insist that God can know the future, yet at the same time we determine our own actions. Are these two possibilities compatible? If so, how? If not, how are we to understand Judaism's insistence on human freedom?

2. a) Rav Saadia asserts that God lets us have complete freedom. How do you understand this claim? Is God holding back in each and every instance, or has God made reality such that God cannot intervene in particular choices we make?

   b) Would our lives be different if God only acted one way or the other? Would God's actions affect our faith?

3. The three medieval sages quoted above—ibn Gabirol, ibn Ezra, and Maimonides—all assert that we can shape our character through the choices we make and the education we open ourselves to. They see us as

responsible for these choices and for our own character formation. Do you agree? Why or why not? How does your stance shape your own life and sense of responsibility?

4. a) Einstein turns the issue of determinism around from one confronting humanity to one confronting the cosmos as a whole. Did the universe have to turn out this way, or were there options not taken? Do you have an answer for Einstein?

   b) Does it matter which scenario occurred?

Resources

Harlow, Jules. *Siddur Sim Shalom: A Prayerbook for Shabbat, Festivals, and Weekdays*. New York: Rabbinical Assembly, 1989.

Heschel, Abraham Joshua. *Man Is Not Alone: A Philosophy of Religion*. New York: Farrar, Straus & Young, 1951.

Hillesum, Etty. *An Interrupted Life: The Diaries 1941–1943; and, Letters from Westerbork*. Translated by Jan G. Gaarlandt. New York: Henry Holt and Company, 1996.

Hirsch, Samson Raphael. *The Nineteen Letters of Ben Uziel: Being a Spiritual Presentation of the Principles of Judaism*. Translated by Bernard Drachman. Whitefish, MT: Kessinger Publishing, 2007.

Holton, Gerald. *The Scientific Imagination: Case Studies*. New York: Cambridge University Press, 1978.

Klein, Joe. "You Believe What!? Theology, Belief, Faith and Religion." *Learning for Its Own Sake*. Accessed November 11, 2014. www.rabbiklein.com/rabbiklein/YouBelieveWhat.html.

Kushner, Harold. "Would an All-Powerful God Be Worthy of Worship?" In *Jewish Theology and Process Thought*, edited by David Ray Griffen and Sandra B. Lubarski, pp. 89–91. Albany, NY: State University of New York Press, 1996.

Levenson, Jon D. *Creation and the Persistence of Evil: The Jewish Drama of Divine Omnipotence*. San Francisco: Harper & Row, 1988.

Maimonides, Moses. *Guide of the Perplexed*. Translated by Shlomo Pines. Chicago: University of Chicago Press, 1963.

———. *Mishneh Torah: A New Translation with Commentaries and Notes*. Translated by Eliyahu Touger. Jerusalem: Moznayim, 1988.

Newman, Louis I., and Samuel Spitz, eds. *The Hasidic Anthology: Tales and Teachings of the Hasidim*. New York: Bloch Publishing Company, 1944.

Rosenzweig, Franz. *On Jewish Learning*. Edited by N. N. Glatzer. New York: Schocken Books, 1955.

Schulweis, Harold. *For Those Who Can't Believe: Overcoming the Obstacles to Faith*. New York: HarperCollins, 1994.

Sommer, Benjamin D. "Revelation at Sinai in the Hebrew Bible and in Jewish Theology." In *The Journal of Religion* 79, no. 3 (1999): 440.

Tucker, Gordon. "Taking in the Torah of the Timeless Present." In *Jewish Mysticism and the Spiritual Life: Classical Texts, Contemporary Reflections*, edited by Lawrence Fine, Eitan P. Fishbane, and Or N. Rose, pp. 67–71. Woodstock, VT: Jewish Lights, 2011.

Rabbi Bradley Shavit Artson, DHL, an inspiring speaker and educator, holds the Abner and Roslyn Goldstine Dean's Chair of the Ziegler School of Rabbinic Studies and is vice president of American Jewish University in Los Angeles. He is a member of the philosophy department, supervises the Miller Introduction to Judaism Program and mentors Camp Ramah in California. He is also dean of Zacharias Frankel College in Potsdam, Germany, ordaining rabbis in Europe. A regular columnist for the *Huffington Post*, he is author of many articles and books, including *Passing Life's Tests: Spiritual Reflections on the Trial of Abraham, the Binding of Isaac* (Jewish Lights). For more teaching resources, visit www.bradartson.com.

Nathan A. Roller is a student at the Zeigler School of Rabbinic Studies in Los Angeles.

Rabbi Artson is available to speak to your group or at your event. For more information, please contact us at (802) 457-4000 or publicity@jewishlights.com.

Praise for *God of Becoming and Relationship: The Dynamic Nature of Process Theology*

"Through honesty, openness and erudition, Rabbi Artson teaches of a God who whispers 'grow' to each of us. A beautiful and soulful exploration."

—**Rabbi David Wolpe**, Sinai Temple, Los Angeles, California; author, *Why Faith Matters*

"Offers us a new way to see ourselves, our world and our God. We no longer have to choose between our faith and our intellect. What a joy and what a relief it is to be able to integrate these seeming disparities. Important…. This is a book that can heal our souls."

—**Rabbi Naomi Levy**, spiritual leader, Nashuva; author, *Hope Will Find You, Talking to God*, and *To Begin Again*

"I wept for joy reading this…. Many of us are wounded by conventional vocabulary when we think and talk about God— our language is stuck, and we are stuck. Artson, one of the most inspiring Jewish leaders and theologians of our time, redeems the ancient covenant of formulating anew our conversation about God."

—**Rabbi Tamar Elad-Appelbaum**, founding rabbi, Zion: An Eretz Israeli Community in Jerusalem

"A pioneering exploration of collaborative ecumenical thinking. Illustrates the complementary and contrasting features in Judaism and Process Theology. In broadening the horizons of the search for wholeness, Artson opens a fantastic adventure of ideas."

—**Rabbi Harold M. Schulweis**, author, *Conscience: The Duty to Obey and the Duty to Disobey*; founder, Jewish Foundation of the Righteous and the Jewish World Watch

"Explicates a twenty-first-century Judaism that is dynamic, constructive, ethical and deeply meaningful; offers ways for us to think about prayer, ritual and Israel, and about what we must do to create greater justice."

—**Ruth W. Messinger**, president, American Jewish World Service

"[A] work of honest struggle by a fellow-seeker for a believable Jewish theology in our day…. Don't miss it!"

—**Arthur Green**, rector, Rabbinical School, Hebrew College

"With personal, persuasive prose … skillfully presents a theology to live with and live by. It may change the way that you think about God, Judaism and your being in the world."

—**Sue Levi Elwell, PhD**, rabbinic director, East Geographic Congregational Network, Union for Reform Judaism

"An amazing combination of personal narrative, introduction to Process Thought and integration of Jewish theology with the two. It should open up to a whole new community the fruitfulness of thinking about God, life and Judaism through Process perspectives."

—**Thomas Jay Oord**, author, *The Nature of Love* and *Defining Love*

"Both a lovely, poetic introduction to Process Theology, and a vivid sense of Rabbi Artson's private journey as a believer, a Jewish leader, a father, a teacher and a Jew…. His enthusiasm and compassion are on every page, inviting you to learn from him and with him."

—**Laurie Zoloth**, director, Center for Bioethics, Science and Society, Northwestern University

"Brings to pass a confluence of Process Theology and Judaism hitherto only hinted at. The vibrant Jewishness of his sources, practices and rhythms of interpretation yield an unsurpassed introduction to the God of becoming—for all children of Sarah, Hagar, Abraham."

—**Catherine Keller**, professor of theology, Drew University; author, *On the Mystery: Discerning Divinity in Process*

"Until now it has been chiefly Protestants who have profited from the brilliant work of Alfred North Whitehead in reformulating ideas about God, the world and our inner lives. Now, in using Whitehead to revitalize Jewish life and thought, Brad Artson outdoes and inspires us all."

—**John B. Cobb Jr.**, professor emeritus, Claremont School of Theology

Printed in the USA
CPSIA information can be obtained
at www.ICGtesting.com
JSHW060056150824
68134JS00032B/2750